THE GREAT BOOK OF

tea

ELAINE LEMM

GREAT N ORTHERN

Great Northern Books
PO Box 213, Ilkley, LS29 9WS
www.greatnorthernbooks.co.uk

ISBN: 978 0 9572951 0 0

Design and layout: David Burrill

Printed in China

CIP Data
A catalogue for this book is available from the British Library

CONTENTS

Introduction

"I like a nice cup of tea in the morning
For to start the day you see
And at half past eleven
Well my idea of heaven
Is a nice cup of tea
I like a nice cup of tea with me dinner
And a nice cup of tea with me tea
And when it's time for bed
There's a lot to be said
For a nice cup of tea"

This well-known song, sung by Binny Hale, precisely sums up the way a cup of tea weaves its way through the British day. Despite only having first put the kettle on for tea in the mid-17th century, tea permeates every part of our lives. This is summed up neatly in the famous tea quote by Marlene Dietrich, "The British have an umbilical cord which has never been cut and through which tea flows constantly".

I cannot remember when I first was given tea to drink, it seems it was always there as part of my daily life and still is. For me, it is the only way to start the day and I can be quite grumpy without it; ask my husband.

It was aged 14, though, when I first realised, not everyone drinks tea. My French penfriend, Brigitte arrived to stay, as part of our school's exchange programme. In my excitement to 'show her off' she was taken to visit a succession of grandparents, aunts, uncles and friends.

By the sixth visit, the poor girl turned a pale shade of green. It seems, she had never drunk tea and given that each time we arrived at yet another house, the kettle went on for tea. She drank

4

a lot of tea that day (being too shy to refuse). It had never crossed my mind that she wouldn't like it; I thought everyone did.

Tea had been the fashion in continental Europe long before it came to Britain and when it did, was so expensive that the first ever sip of tea was reserved only for the rich. A mere century later, thanks to reforms in the extortionate tax on tea, it also became a drink of the working classes. They cast aside their morning draught of beer and turned to tea, thanks in part to the restorative properties of the morning cuppa.

Before not too long, there were tea breaks in the workplace with of course tea and biscuits, tea shops on the high street, tea gardens, parties and dances. Tea was drunk not only in the morning but at lunch, dinner and Afternoon Tea became the best of all treats. Tea appeared in literature (try reading Dickens or Austen without finding a mention of it) in song and in art.

Tea's ability to revive flagging spirits makes it the first port of call in times of crisis, sadness and as a curative, with a cup of sweet tea for shock. And, not forgetting the great pleasure of putting the kettle on when friends or family drop by.

Tea is used as a medicine, in beauty treatments, to ward off evil spirits and to predict the future. However, above all, with 162 million cups of tea drunk in Britain every day (only Ireland tops the British as tea drinkers), it is the national drink.

In the British class-ridden society, both past and present, the cup of tea has smartly managed to cross any divide and whether you put milk in first or last, thankfully no longer holds any social affectation. From the 'builder's brew' to the finest oolong's, we simply love tea and life in Britain without it would be unimaginable. Makes me wonder if tea is actually in the British DNA?

Elaine Lemm *July 2012*

Acknowledgements

Life in Britain without tea is unthinkable, so thanks must go firstly to everyone across the centuries, who worked assiduously to bring tea to these shores. Equally, a huge thanks also to Anna, Duchess of Bedford; had it not been for her hunger pangs, that most British of customs, the Afternoon Tea would not exist.

Writing this book would have been much more difficult without the help of the following: the British Tea Council for the fascinating facts and figures; Jonathan Jones and Abby Keverne at Tregothnan Tea for inviting me to the beautiful Tregothnan Estate in Cornwall; both The Ritz and Fortnum and Mason in London for their help and support. To the outstanding team at Bettys and Taylors, in Harrogate, big thanks, especially to Laura for her help in making things happen and to Ian Brabbin for teaching me to taste tea properly and opening my eyes to the fascinating world of the tea buyer.

My lovely stepdaughter continues to weave her magic in the kitchen, thank you for sharing your recipes and your help with the photography. Sister Liz, big thanks for 'taking the load' while I got on with this and Irene for the chasing and organising. Yvonne, you are a trouper and have no idea what I would do without you and that's not just the proofreading.

Finally, to my husband Ron. Sometimes I forget to say thank you for your love and support and the cuppa you bring me every, single morning; it is my favourite of the day. And, of course, for the beautiful photography.

What is Tea?

Tea is a hot drink made from pouring boiling water over dried leaves. Despite hundreds of products labelled tea, to be the 'real thing', those leaves must come from the *Camellia Sinensis*, the tea plant, which looks not unlike a privet hedge. Just like fine wine, many factors can affect the finished tea. The soil, the altitude and climate have an effect, as does the ways the leaves are harvested, fermented, roasted and blended. Hence, the myriad of teas found on sale.

There are three common varieties of tea available, white, green and black, and all start with the green leaves which are then processed differently. Black teas are created from heavily fermented leaves and the most popular tea for everyday drinking. White teas are the tips of the unopened leaves which are dried with no fermentation, resulting in a light, delicate and expensive tea. Green tea lies somewhere between the two.

All three have roughly the same levels of caffeine, but the unfermented white tea has higher levels of antioxidants and nutrients.

A Brief History of Tea

The Beginnings

Tea is, and has been, synonymous with Britain and Ireland for so long that understandably, many think this is where it all began. No. Our association with tea is but a mere 350 years old: it is to China, 4750 years ago we must go to for the origins.

Separating out legend from fact is difficult but a few wild leaves falling into a pot of boiling water seems to be the accepted beginning. It was Chinese Emperor Shen Nung boiling the water and who, coincidentally, was also a scholar and herbalist.

"It quenches thirst," he declared. "It lessens the desire for sleep. It gladdens the heart."

Stories of this type abound across the centuries: all profess to a love of tea, health benefits and tea's ability to stimulate the mind and the senses.

It was during the Han Dynasty (206 -220 AD) that tea became popular and by the third century AD, China's national drink. Moving forward another 500 years and China's first tea specialist, LuYu published Ch'a Chang (Classic of Tea). It took 20 years to write and became the essential work for tea farmers, merchants, and tea drinkers. At the time, tea was also on the move, spreading from China, into Tibet, to the West and beyond.

It was not until the latter end of the sixteenth century that tea was mentioned in Europe. It is believed to have been brought from China by returning Portuguese merchants and missionaries along with silks and spices. Commercial trade in tea though, started with the Dutch, who, having established a trading post on the island of Java, shipped the first consignment of tea from China to Holland in 1606. From Holland, the drinking of tea spread into continental Europe but as prices were very high, was a drink only for the wealthy.

Catherine of Braganza

Tea in Britain

Britain had rejected the continental fashion for tea drinking, so finding tea in Britain in the mid-late seventeenth century, though available, was unusual.

Thomas Garraway sold tea in his general store in London and in 1660 wrote a broadsheet named *An Exact Description of the Growth, Quality and Vertes of the Leaf Tea.*

As well as where it comes from and how it is produced, he states 14 reasons why tea was good for you, including a cure for headaches, skin complaints, kidney problems, infections and scurvy.

In the same year, diarist Samuel Pepys makes mention after discussing foreign affairs with friends:

'And afterwards did send for a Cupp of Tee (a China drink) of which I never drank before'.

The turning point for tea came in 1662 when the Portuguese princess, Catherine of Braganza, arrived in Britain for her marriage to King Charles II and included a chest of tea in her dowry as she was a big fan, having grown up drinking tea. Slowly, tea became a fashionable drink, but as it was heavily taxed by the government, was seen only in courtly and aristocratic circles.

One consequence of the heavy taxation on tea was the increase of ways to avoid it. The rising demand for tea across the social classes meant many could not afford the precious commodity and a 'black-market' evolved. The small illegal trade soon developed into an organised crime network using brutal methods to supply the growing demand. At its height as much as 7 million pounds annually were illegally imported and often the tea was adulterated with dried leaves from other plants.

Eventually, it became apparent that the tax was not worth the problems it created and in 1784 Prime Minister William Pitt the Younger slashed the tax from 119% to 12.5% making tea affordable and the smuggling ceased.

By the middle of the eighteenth century, the breakfast drink of ale and beer were cast aside as tea became the preferred drink of all classes in Britain. From the cuppa in the workplace, the tea allowance for household servants and the free tea for workers - which would eventually become the tea-break in the 20th century - through to the serving of tea in the most elegant homes, the British embraced tea. Consequently, it is believed that as the water for tea is boiled, the drinking of tea reduced urban disease and illness thus fuelling the industrial revolution.

Relations with China deteriorated in the early part of the 19th century and new supplies of tea were needed. It was a new variety of tea bush growing in northern India which came to the rescue. The first imports of Assam tea arrived just in time as Britain declared war on China in 1839 and no Chinese tea was imported again until 1860.

Though previously a coffee growing region, Ceylon also began to grow very good tea around the 1870s and joined by the teas from India became the preferred flavours for tea in Britain and the popularity of China tea declined.

The approach to tea during the two World Wars bears testament to the importance of the morale-boosting beverage to the British way of life. The government took over the importation of tea to ensure that the beverage was available and affordable to everyone during the First, and rationed tea from 1940 to 1952 in the Second.

Through the second half of the 20th century, tea has held its own despite the popularity of the American coffee shop chains, skinny mochas and brownies. Into the 21st century tea is enjoying something of a revival especially with niche connoisseur teas. The popularity of green, oolong and speciality teas is growing and tea is once again being recognised for its health properties. It is now acknowledged that tea is healthier, as it contains less caffeine than coffee and, like fruit and vegetables, tea is a natural source of

polyphenols and flavonoids which have antioxidant activity.

A staggering 162 million cups are still drunk every day in Britain so, happily, it seems the British love of tea is as strong today as it ever was.

Tea ration book

Bringing Tea Home

A Royal charter in 1600 by Queen Elizabeth gave the monopoly for all British trade with the Indies to the East India Company. However, until 1669, any tea brought into Britain was imported by the Dutch East Indies Company. To begin with, imports of tea by the British company were slow starting with a meager 143 lbs, and imports remained steady until 1678, when the market was swamped with tea. This continued until the end of the century, when tea drinking took off with a vengeance and demand rocketed. By 1750 annual imports reached 4,727,992 lbs.

The East India Company retained their monopoly on the tea trade until 1834. Without competition the company took their time importing the tea despite demand. A round trip could take anything up to two years. All that changed when tea became a free trade.

Speed was paramount to supplying the rising demand, and whoever arrived home first bagged the best price for their precious cargo and coincidentally, supplied the market with a fresher product. The ships, therefore, needed to be lighter, sleeker and faster. The Americans pioneered what became known as the Clipper Ship (named for the way they clipped off the miles on a voyage).

The first true Clipper, *Rainbow*, was launched in 1845 with the first British Clipper in the 1850s. There was a great spirit of competition between America and Britain with Clipper Races, each vying to bring the cargo home faster, to earn that extra sum.

Their glory days proved to be short-lived with the opening of the Suez Canal in 1869. With the navigable passage between the Far East and the Mediterranean the journey was cut dramatically; steam ships until this time were not viable for transporting tea – they required humongous storage space for the coal needed to fuel the ships, leaving little room for any other cargo. The glamorous ships disappeared with only one, *The Cutty Sark*, still surviving in the world and can be seen at Greenwich Dock in London.

The Boston Tea Party

Throughout the 18th century tea was popular in Britain's American colonies as at home. All tea coming into America had to come through Britain, but an Act of Parliament in 1773 gave a monopoly to the East India Company. The Tea Act as it was known was deemed a way to rescue the finances of the once successful company now suffering because of tea smuggling. A 3d per lb tax was levied, which coincidentally was a lot less than the current tax on tea in Britain, but was a tax too far for the colonists.

The Americans, already angered at being taxed by a remote parliament, had previously boycotted many British imports, but now objected to the tea being supplied only by the East India Company; a move that would surely put American tea merchants out of business. They decided not to pay the 3d tax.

Despite the resistance, the East India Company sent 4 ships – the

Dartmouth, Eleanor, Beaver and *William* to Boston fully laden with their cargo of tea.

Three of the ships arrived in Boston (the William had run aground in Cape Cod) but the townspeople refused to unload the cargo. The ships could not return to Britain with the tea, as customs officers had completed the paperwork for the import. With the impasse, the ships languished in the harbour.

Meetings and avid discussions failed and on the night of December 16th, 1773, a band of men, some disguised as Mohawk American Indians, assembled on the wharf. With cries of 'The Mohawks are coming' and 'Boston harbour, a teapot tonight', they boarded the ships and within three hours, 340 tea chests were forced open and thrown overboard. There was no violence and nothing else on the ships was damaged.

The error of judgement by the British and the defiance of the colonists led to the American War of Independence and to Britain's subsequent loss of the American colonies.

Afternoon Tea – A Very British Custom

There is no more quintessential British ritual than the ceremony and serving of Afternoon Tea. It is believed that credit for the custom goes to Anna, the 7th Duchess of Bedford in the early 19th century. The usual habit of serving dinner between 8 and 9 pm left the Duchess hungry and with a 'sinking feeling' by late afternoon. To stave off the hunger, she would order tea, bread and butter and cakes to be served in her room. Later on she would invite friends to join her at her home and the light tea was such a success, the habit caught on.

The Duchess continued the custom on returning to London and soon the 'At Home' tea evolved which quickly spread throughout England. Announcements about tea were sent to relatives and friends stating at what hour the tea would be served. Sometimes entertainment was provided, but more often it was simply conversation and a little idle gossip over tea and cakes. If 'At Home' notices were received the guest was expected to attend, unless of course, regrets were sent. There was at least one person holding an at home each day and social ties were quickly established with women seeing each other so regularly.

The taking of tea gradually spread from the home and out into society in general. Tea parties became the norm and Tea Rooms, and Tea Gardens quickly sprang up everywhere.

During the Edwardian period, the 'At Home' faded as the fashion to travel increased. Tea was now served in the new tea lounges of luxury hotels and was often accompanied by light music and sometimes even a little dancing.

The two World Wars radically changed the taking of Afternoon Tea, especially with tea rationing continuing into the 50s, but the custom did survive, only just. As the British began their love affair with coffee bars in the 1960s, sadly, Afternoon Tea became little more than a morsel of faded British tradition to dangle before tourists.

Whizzing forward to the 21st century though, how come Afternoon Tea at the Ritz is now one of the hardest-to-book dining experiences in London? And, outside the famous Bettys Tea Rooms in Yorkshire, queues circle the block. Come 3 o'clock, up and down the country, hotel dining rooms are full and tables groan under the weight of stands, jam-packed with cakes and scones. Teas are back once again and in a big way.

Ironically, it is the economic downturn which began around 2008 that is credited for this revival. The return to more traditional values and homely pursuits is more prevalent when money is tight, it seems.

There is one big difference, however. In the Duchess' time, tea neatly filled a gap in the day. Today, the afternoon repast tends both to replace lunch and diminish the need for a large dinner. Afternoon Tea is a way to meet and eat and what better way to use up time on a wet, cold 'staycation', than a few hours lingering over tea and scones? So fashionable is Afternoon Tea that brides on a budget are choosing to serve it instead of the formal sit-down meal.

Examples from The Ritz (top left) and Fortnum and Mason.

17

What is Served at Afternoon Tea?

The Afternoon Tea traditionally starts with savoury finger-sized sandwiches filled with smoked salmon, cucumber, or egg and mustard cress. These are followed by scones with jam and cream (clotted cream in Devon and Cornwall), and finally, a selection of cakes served on tiered cake stands. Variations on the menu may include the serving of English muffins, thinly sliced, hot-buttered toast or crumpets.

Alongside of course, are copious cups of tea. The tea is traditionally poured from heavy, ornate, silver teapots into delicate bone-china cups and served with milk or lemon.

High Tea

The origins of the Afternoon Tea show clearly this was the preserve of the rich in the 19th century. For workers in the newly industrialised Britain of the time, 'tea' had to wait until after work and be substantially more than just tea and cakes. Workers needed sustenance following a day of hard labour, so the after-work meal was more often hot and filling, accompanied by a pot of good, strong tea to revive flagging spirits. Additionally, the word 'High' differentiates between the Afternoon Tea served on low, comfortable, parlour chairs or relaxing in the garden and the worker's meal served at the table, seated on high back dining chairs.

Today, the evening meal in working class households is sometimes still called 'Tea' but as working patterns have changed yet again, many households now refer to the evening meal as supper.

Afternoon Tea in Wales

Renowned author and authority on Welsh food Gilli Davies, describes the differences between a Welsh to an English Afternoon Tea, and essentially it comes down to two things:

Welsh Cakes and Bara Brith

According to Gilli Davies, Lloyd George had a fondness for pancakes which in Wales are particularly good. Stacked thick and high, straight off the griddle and oozing with melted butter, you can just imagine a Welsh tea served before the open fire. The griddle constantly played an important part in Celtic cookery, with Welsh cakes being the Welsh speciality (See recipe on page 76). These sweet griddled scones are very moreish and it's always difficult to stop at eating just one. In the past they were sometimes cooked in a 'Dutch Oven' which sat in the embers of the fire and here too the miner's cake, Teisen Lap, would be baked; a moist cake to take down the pit, which wasn't dry and crumbly.

Once ovens were available, a weekly bread bake became the norm, and many a housewife would add a few currants to the last lump of bread dough to make a delicious tea bread, known as Bara Brith or literally – speckled bread (recipe on page 87). Spread thickly with farm butter and a chunk of Caerphilly cheese, it is delicious!

Gilli is the author of the renowned book of Welsh food, Flavours of Wales, published by Graffeg, which was nominated for a Gourmand World Book Award 2012.

Afternoon Tea in Scotland

Without doubt, Scotland more than anywhere in the United Kingdom, eschews the dainty Afternoon Tea for something a little more substantial. The Scottish reference to tea is not the drink but more akin to the High Tea served in Northern England. According to Sue Lawrence, the distinguished Scottish food writer, it consists of a hefty savoury dish (eggs, smoked fish or in summer, a salad) served with bread and butter, followed by scones (be they plain, treacle or potato), cakes and buns. Expect a Selkirk Bannock and a rich, dense Dundee fruit cake to make an appearance. According to Sue, tea will invariably take place between 5 and 6 o'clock.

The lighter Afternoon Tea served south of the Scottish border is also served in Scotland; it is simply that the difference between the two must be made clear lest anyone expecting the substantial High Tea feels cheated.

Cornish or Devon Cream Tea

A cream tea from the south west consists of little more than freshly baked scones, fruity jam, clotted cream and a pot of tea.

The clotted cream originates in the south west and is a silky, yellow cream with a distinctive crust on the surface. It is made by heating unpasteurized cow's milk, which then is left in a shallow pan for many hours. This causes the cream to rise to the surface and 'clot'.

Arguments abound between Devon and Cornwall as to the true home of the 'Cream Tea' and while there is no answer, there are subtle differences between them; in Devon, cream then jam on the scone; in Cornwall, jam first followed by cream.

Tregothnan Tea, Britain's only Tea Plantation

Tea growing is more often associated with far-off continents and tropical climates but is also, surprisingly, grown in Britain, at Tregothnan, near Truro in Cornwall, to be precise.

The Tregothnan estate is not just Britain's only tea plantation, it is also home to the Boscawen Family and seat of the Viscounts Falmouth since 1335. Despite having the largest historic gardens in Cornwall, Tregothnan is a private estate and not open to the public except for a limited number of private garden tours and an annual Open Weekend. Each April, the estate opens for charity, and attracts thousands of visitors who flock in to explore the 40 hectares of stunning gardens and see the collections of magnificent magnolias, camellias and rhododendrons.

The estate is also an official 'safe site' for the keeping of rare or endangered trees and plants from all over the world. At Tregothnan is the world's only surviving travelling greenhouse and a fascinating Wollemi pine or 'Dinosaur tree' - a prehistoric species thought to be extinct until 1994, when a handful of trees was discovered in a remote Australian valley.

Above all, Tregothnan is a working estate. Besides the tea, the estate produces Kea plum jam, (the damson-like Kea plums peculiar to the area), biscuits, estate honeys and seasonal British flowers which are sold to the floristry trade and direct to the public.

It was the camellias, all but growing wild at Tregothnan, which first sparked head gardener Jonathan Jones into considering growing the tea bushes. The camellia thrived on the estate so why not the *Camellia Sinensis* (the tea bush). The pocket of Cornwall off the Fal estuary has a warm micro-climate, the right soil and amount of rainfall in which the bush thrives. It was not an easy ride and the first crop was a disaster but just over a decade after planting - and a substantial financial investment - the first cup of Tregothnan Classic blend tea was sold in 2006. The plantation now turns over £1 million per year in tea and a rapidly growing reputation for fine tea, tea blends and infusions.

Tea is available to buy on line at www.tregothnanshop.co.uk

"Wouldn't it be dreadful to live in a country where they didn't have tea?"
Noel Coward

Famous Names in British Tea

Through the centuries, there are many names synonymous with the world of tea in Britain. Here are just a few of the more famous, and my particular favourites.

Yorkshire Tea

No book of tea, for me, would be complete without tea from my home county. It is the tea I wake up to every morning, including when I travel, as I take it with me. I am not the only fan it seems, as the tea has something of a celebrity following too, including Noel Gallagher and Ozzy Osbourne. Look closely at any box of Yorkshire Tea and you will see The Royal Warrant of Appointment which was granted to Taylors of Harrogate by The Prince of Wales for supplying his London residence, Clarence House.

It is brothers Charles Edward and Llewellyn Taylor who, in 1886, set up their tea and coffee importing business, with Charles opening tea and coffee 'Kiosks' with tasting rooms attached, in the thriving spa towns of Harrogate and Ilkley. The 'Kiosks' went on to enjoy huge success, with the tasting rooms eventually becoming cafés. The business thrived well into the 20th Century, but in the 60s with no family heir to carry on the business, Taylors was put up for sale. From an overheard conversation in another of Harrogate's famous tea shops, Bettys, that Taylors were selling both their tea shops and their tea and coffee importing business, a buyer was found. Bettys bought Taylors and the newly formed company of Bettys and Taylors went on to become one of Yorkshire's most famous and loved brands.

Taylors of Harrogate Tea Blends

The most celebrated *Yorkshire Tea* blend is described perfectly by Taylors as "A proper brew. Pure and simple."

Yorkshire Gold is a luxury blend of second flush of peak season Assam and East African teas.

And, living as I do in a hard water area, my favourite is *Yorkshire Tea for Hard Water*, the only tea specially blended to suit local tap water.

Earl Grey

Charles, 2nd Earl Grey was British Prime Minister from 1830 to 1834 and is famed for managing to pass The Great Reform Bill of 1832, which started the process of parliamentary reform, leading eventually to modern British democracy.

The Earl lived at Howick Hall in Northumberland. The distinctive-tasting Earl Grey tea (named after the Earl) was specially blended by a Chinese mandarin who used Bergamot to offset the lime-tasting water in the well at Howick. The tea became popular when Lady Grey served it in London and was eventually marketed by Twinings and now sells worldwide. Sadly, the Greys didn't register the trademark, so never received a penny in royalties for the tea.

Twinings

Twinings is one of the oldest tea brands in Britain. The renowned tea company dates back to 1706 when the far-thinking Thomas Twining, tired of drinking ale in the morning (which was common practice at the time), started selling tea from his coffee house on London's Strand. He quickly gained many fans of the 'new' beverage and its restorative qualities, including Jane Austen and Charles II.

Despite great opposition from the pub owners seeing profits dwindle, and heavy tea taxation, he persisted and opened the Golden Lyon, Britain's first tea shop. Three hundred years later, as well as still selling tea from Thomas's shop, the tea is sold worldwide except now there are over 100 varieties.

Ringtons Tea

Ringtons is a family business that started life in 1907, when Samuel Smith left Leeds and began selling tea from a horse and carriage to households in Heaton, Newcastle upon Tyne. Within a year, Sam needed two horses and four assistants, so rapid was the expansion of his business.

By the 20s the motor vehicle had arrived and Ringtons bought two in the hope of improving the speed of deliveries. It was not popular with the Geordie tea drinkers, they preferred the horses and cart and it was another 40 years before the last horse retired.

Eventually Sam returned to Leeds and in the 1930s opened the Ringtons factory, and the family-run business went from strength to strength. In the 21st century, Ringtons still deliver door-to-door to over 280,000 customers, worldwide to many more from the on-line shop and has a thriving wholesale business, including selling to Marks and Spencer.

Other Large Brands

There are many, many other brands marketing and selling tea in Britain. See page 93 for the more niche suppliers. Many long-standing tea companies have been swallowed up by large international conglomerates but still remain an intrinsic part of British tea heritage. Who can forget the chimps of P G Tips tea, the cartoon tea graders over at Tetley's or the picture cards from Brooke Bond.

Famous Afternoon Tea Venues

Say Afternoon Tea and certain names instantly spring to mind: The Ritz and Fortnum and Mason (just 2 of the many) in London; Bettys in the North; The Balmoral in Edinburgh and skip across to Ireland for a very special tea in Dublin at the Merrion Hotel. The recent revival of Afternoon Tea means it is now available, not just across Britain and Ireland, but around the world.

The Ritz, London

Probably the most famous venue for Afternoon Tea in Britain is the Ritz in London. The renowned hotel opened in 1906 and has remained a firm favourite ever since. So popular is Afternoon Tea in the luxury and grandeur of the Palm Court at the Ritz, that booking needs to be made up to three months in advance.

Expect a selection of 17 different teas and a traditional range of Afternoon Tea foods; freshly cut sandwiches; warm scones served with jam and cream; tea cakes and pastries, served by tuxedo-clad waiters.

A resident pianist, performs renditions of Afternoon Tea traditional tunes, including, of course, 'Puttin' on The Ritz' and 'A Nightingale Sang in Berkeley Square'.

As it would be expected at a hotel of this calibre, the dress code at the Ritz is strict; gentlemen are required to wear a jacket and tie; jeans, sportswear and trainers are not permitted.

Fortnum and Mason

Since Fortnum and Mason set up their renowned store over three hundred years ago – the first delivery of tea in 1720 – right through to today, Fortnum's has been synonymous with high quality tea in Britain and an important purveyor of tea to the wealthy and well-to-do.

In 1926, the store was transformed into a department store with a restaurant offering afternoon tea and continued as such until in March 2012, in celebration of the Queen's Diamond Jubilee, Fortnum and Mason opened the doors of their own jewel: The Diamond Jubilee Tea Salon.

Out went the St James's Restaurant, and in came a décor fit for the 21st century and reflecting Fortnum's Georgian origins, whilst capturing the elegant, peaceful atmosphere through the rest of the store. And, the first customers to take afternoon tea in the Diamond Jubilee Salon, HM the Queen accompanied by Their Royal Highnesses the Duchess of Cornwall and the Duchess of Cambridge.

As would be expected, there is an extensive tea menu on offer of

around 75 teas, from Fortnum's own blends to very rare and unusual teas, the ubiquitous scones, jam and cream and an elegant array of cakes, tarts and patisserie.

The Merrion, Dublin

The 5-star, Georgian hotel in Dublin, serves what is considered the most lavish afternoon tea in Dublin City, with an unusual slice of 19th and 20th-century art inspired by the work of J.B Yeats, William Scott and Louis Le Brocquy - to name a few.

Tea is served in the elegant drawing room of the hotel and contains all the usual suspects of tea, but it is the arrival of exquisite, miniature, sweet creations based on paintings found at the hotel, which make this an unusual and inspirational tea.

From Plant to Pot

The *Camellia Sinensis* (tea plant) enjoys a warm, humid climate with temperatures ranging from 10 – 35 °C. It needs a decent amount of rainfall and prefers a deep, light, acidic and well-drained soil. With the right conditions, the tea plant will grow anywhere from sea-level up to altitudes of 2100m.

Newly planted young shrubs are left untouched for two years before any pruning or plucking, but once old enough, are pruned to keep them under a metre high. This neat pruning means as new shoots appear, known as a 'flush', they are easily visible to the pickers. It is these young green leaves which are used in tea production. Different plucks produce different qualities of tea; in Darjeeling the 1st flush is considered the best; in Assam, it is the 2nd.

The delicate shoots are grasped lightly between the tip of the

thumb and middle finger and in a deft, downward movement broken off and thrown over the shoulder into baskets on the picker's back. Dependent on the location and of the tea plantation, plucking can take place every 7 – 14 days. Given that smaller leaves found in Darjeeling requires 22,000 shoots per kilo of tea, or Assam where they are larger, 10,000, this is painstaking work. Sometimes a skilled worker will use shears and there is machinery to trim the shoots, but as these will also include bits of stem and wood, produce a lower grade tea.

The leaves are then taken into the factory, spread onto large trays and racks and left to wither in warm air. Once withered, the flaccid leaves are broken by rollers to release the juices and enzymes of the plant, which, as they come into contact with the air, oxidise. The broken leaves are laid out in a cool, humid atmosphere for several hours to ferment or oxidise, until eventually the leaves turn golden and oxidisation is complete. Finally, the oxidised leaves are dried completely, which further changes the colour of the leaves to black. The tea is now 'made' – the technical name meaning the tea is now ready.

The tea is then sorted into varying sizes before being weighed and packed into tea chests. Along the way the factory tea tasters will check the flavour of the tea to make sure it is not contaminated, and once satisfied, samples will be sent to brokers to be evaluated for quality and of course, price.

This method of processing varies for different teas:

Green Tea: the withered leaf is steamed and rolled before drying to prevent the leaves from breaking and causing oxidisation.

White Tea: the buds are hand-plucked and are withered so the natural moisture evaporates before drying. No oxidisation takes place.

Oolong Tea: is a cross between a black and green tea, with a much shorter oxidisation, making it a fresh tasting tea but with sophisticated nuances of a black.

A Day in the Life of a Tea Taster

If you think being a professional tea buyer involves sitting around drinking endless cups of tea all day, you may want to think again. Their role is far more complex as I learned on a tea tutorial with Ian Brabbin, head of tea at Taylors of Harrogate.

The tea buyers at Taylors taste as many as 1100 teas in a single day. They sift through the samples which arrive from tea gardens around the world, to identify where the best teas are coming from. As these teas go on to be part of the Yorkshire Tea blend, consistency for the consumer is paramount . The quality of tea can change daily on the estates, so it is important to taste a lot to ensure the flavour of the blend always remains the same.

Both the flavour and the body of the tea are important but are not the only aspects which come under their scrutiny; the appearance of the leaves both before and after brewing is also imperative in helping to define the quality.

Brewing the tea for tasting

All teas to be tasted must first be brewed in a very specific way and brewed to double strength to intensify the characteristics of the tea.

5.6g of tea is placed in special lidded tea cups. The tea is then brewed for 5 ½ minutes using freshly drawn and boiled water. Alongside, the dry tea leaf is also displayed

Immediately the timer goes off, the tea cups are tipped, allowing the tea (called liquor in the tea tasting room) to flow into the cup through the serrated edges; this filters out the leaves which are then placed onto the lid.

Finally, milk is added, making sure the same amount goes into each cup.

Tasting the tea

The tea tasting room then becomes a noisy place!

To taste tea involves engaging the 9000 taste buds on the tongue. The tea is slurped (quite literally, making a rather loud, sharp slurping sound) thus spraying the taste buds and also sucking in a good volume of oxygen which also helps define the taste.

Once swirled the tea is spat out into a spittoon. Words to describe the tea fly around the tea tasting room; coloury, complex, flavoury, bright, bakey, brassy; it's a language all of its own.

Easy as this may sound it takes 2 years to develop the palate in order to properly taste tea as there are many aspects to be considered in both the flavour and body of the tea.

Tasting tea, however, is not the only role for the team. At Taylors they will also be involved in managing the supply chain from bush to cup, negotiating with suppliers, buying the teas and creating the blends.

The buyers travel extensively as Taylors are committed to trading ethically and maintain a very close, personal and long-standing relationship (some going back generations) with all their suppliers. They work closely with them to ensure they are socially and environmentally responsible.

There is no typical day in this job it seems; one day slurping in Harrogate another in Kenya, Assam or any one of the many other countries which go to make up Yorkshire Tea.

Earl Grey
[CAMELLIA SINENSIS & CITRUS BERGAMIA]

Darjeeling
[CAMELLIA SINENSIS]

Assam
[CAMELLIA ASSAMICA]

Ceylon O.P.
[CAMELLIA SINENSIS]

Pu Erh
[CAMELLIA SINENSIS]

Genmaicha
[CAMELLIA SINENSIS & GENMAI]

Sencha
[CAMELLIA SINENSIS]

Kukicha
[CAMELLIA SINENSIS]

Keemun
[CAMELLIA SINENSIS]

Pai Mu Tan
[CAMELLIA SINENSIS]

Formosa Gunpowder
[CAMELLIA SINENSIS]

Lapsang Souchong
[CAMELLIA SINENSIS]

Aphrodisiac Tea
[PERFUMED CAMELLIA SINENSIS]

Formosa Oolong
[CAMELLIA SINENSIS]

Kenya Marinyn
[CAMELLIA SINENSIS]

Bengal Fire
[CAMELLIA SINENSIS & SPICES]

Mu Tea
[SIXTEEN WILD HERBS]

Chai Tea
[CAMELLIA SINENSIS & SPICES]

Tea Flower
[CAMELLIA SINENSIS & SPICES]

Green Rooibos
[ASPALATHUS LINEARIS]

Which Tea?

With over 1500 different teas available, choosing the right one may seem complicated but is actually quite straightforward.

The black, white, green and oolong teas each can vary in flavour and nuance dependent on where they come from, how they are grown and processed.

India, Sri Lanka and Africa are renowned for their black tea, Japan for their green and China all 4.

Popular Indian Teas

Darjeeling which comes from Northern India and is a light delicate tea – perfect for Afternoon Teas.

Assam, in north-east India produces a strong, malty tea which stands up well to being blended.

Ceylon Tea is slightly stronger than Darjeeling. It is aromatic with a slightly sharp taste.

Popular Chinese

Lapsang Souchong is perhaps the most famous of China teas, the best coming from the hills in north Fujian. It has a smoky aroma and flavour.

Yunnan is a black tea from the province of Yunnan. The rich, earthy flavour is similar to Assam and makes a great breakfast tea.

White Tea is renowned in China. There are 4 main varieties: Silver Needle (Baihao Yinzhen), White Peony (Bai Mudan), Long Life Eyebrow (Shou Mei), and Tribute Eyebrow (Gong Mei). The tea has a light, delicate, slightly sweet flavour. With less caffeine than other teas, and much less processing, it is considered a healthy tea to drink.

Besides these 4 big players, tea also comes from many countries in the world, where the climatic, and growing conditions prevail, including in south-west Britain on the Tregothnan Estate.

How to Make the Perfect Cup of Tea

Everyone it seems has an opinion on the perfect cup of tea. Here are just 3, all of which have a few points in common; use freshly boiled water, let the tea stand, add milk, the rest it seems is personal preference.

The tea expert's method

1. Warm the pot.

Whether using tea bags or leaf, a quick swirl of hot water means the cold doesn't shock the tea.

2. Use a china teapot.

Why, because it is traditional and part of the ritual.

3. One spoon per person and one for the pot.

Still the golden rule when using a loose-leaf tea.

4. Freshly boiled water.

Boil the water fresh, (not reboiled) for good oxygen levels.

5. Stir.

Stirring the tea leaves or bags helps the tea to infuse.

6. The Time

3 – 4 minutes is the time needed for optimum infusion.

7. Milk?

Milk first or last is an age-old question. Originally milk first was to avoid cracking delicate china cups with hot tea, but adding milk after is a good way to judge the strength of the tea. However, it is each to their own.

Based on advice from the professional tea buyer for Taylors of Harrogate.

The scientist's point of view

Research published in 2011 reveals that scientists at Northumbria's School of Life Science have discovered that the key to the best-tasting brew is to let it sit for six minutes before drinking. Allowing the tea to rest this way avoids it scolding as it has cooled to 60°C, apparently the optimum temperature for the flavours to flow. However, leave it 17 minutes and 30 seconds and the tea will be past its best.

Their conclusion was to add boiling water to a tea bag in a mug and leave for two minutes. Remove the bag, add the milk and leave for a further six minutes or until it reaches 60°C. Should the temperature drop below 45°C the flavours are destroyed.

Taste tests reported dominant 'flavour notes' of wood and grass in black or over-brewed tea, together with hints of lemon, rose and geranium. However, adding milk significantly reduced these notes, replacing them with toffee and vanilla. The more milk added, the more the sweeter notes intensified.

'This may explain why 98% of Brits love tea with milk,' Mr Brown, a food and nutrition expert, said.

Instructions for the perfect cup of tea for one:

1. Add 200ml of freshly boiled water to your tea bag (in a mug).

2. Allow the tea bag to brew for 2 minutes.

3. Remove the tea bag.

4. Add 10ml of milk.

5. Wait 6 minutes before consumption for the cuppa to reach its optimum temperature of 60° centigrade.

The Writer's Opinion

A musing ripe for debate comes from George Orwell in 1946. Tea at this time was still rationed but that doesn't stop him and his dictates on strong tea. Otherwise, he has some valid points.

George Orwell's Musings on Making a Cup of Tea

First published in The Evening Standard, *January 12th, 1946*

First of all, one should use Indian or Ceylonese tea. China tea has virtues which are not to be despised nowadays — it is economical, and one can drink it without milk — but there is not much stimulation in it. One does not feel wiser, braver or more optimistic after drinking it. Anyone who has used that comforting phrase 'a nice cup of tea' invariably means Indian tea.

Secondly, tea should be made in small quantities — that is, in a teapot. Tea out of an urn is always tasteless, while army tea, made in a cauldron, tastes of grease and whitewash. The teapot should be made of china or earthenware. Silver or Britanniaware teapots produce inferior tea and enamel pots are worse; though curiously enough, a pewter teapot (a rarity nowadays) is not so bad.

Thirdly, the pot should be warmed beforehand. This is better done by placing it on the hob than by the usual method of swilling it out with hot water.

Fourthly, the tea should be strong. For a pot holding a quart, if you are going to fill it nearly to the brim, six heaped teaspoons would be about right. In a time of rationing, this is not an idea that can be realized on every day of the week, but I maintain that one strong cup of tea is better than twenty weak ones. All true tea lovers not only like their tea strong, but like it a little stronger with each year that passes — a fact which is recognized in the extra ration issued to old-age pensioners.

Fifthly, the tea should be put straight into the pot. No strainers, muslin bags or other devices to imprison the tea. In some countries teapots are fitted with little dangling baskets under the spout to catch the stray leaves, which are supposed to be harmful. Actually one can swallow tea-leaves in considerable quantities without ill effect, and if the tea is not loose in the pot it never infuses properly.

Sixthly, one should take the teapot to the kettle and not the other way about. The water should be actually boiling at the moment of impact, which means that one should keep it on the flame while one pours. Some people add that one should only use water that has been freshly brought to the boil, but I have never noticed that it makes any difference.

Seventhly, after making the tea, one should stir it, or better, give the pot a good shake, afterwards allowing the leaves to settle.

Eighthly, one should drink out of a good breakfast cup — that is, the cylindrical type of cup, not the flat, shallow type. The breakfast cup holds more, and with the other kind one's tea is always half cold before one has well started on it.

Ninthly, one should pour the cream off the milk before using it for tea. Milk that is too creamy always gives tea a sickly taste.

Tenthly, one should pour tea into the cup first. This is one of the most controversial points of all; indeed in every family in Britain there are probably two schools of thought on the subject. The milk-first school can bring forward some fairly strong arguments, but I maintain that my own argument is unanswerable. This is that, by putting the tea in first and stirring as one pours, one can exactly regulate the amount of milk whereas one is liable to put in too much milk if one does it the other way round.

Lastly, tea — unless one is drinking it in the Russian style — should be drunk without sugar. I know very well that I am in a minority here. But still, how can you call yourself a true tea-lover if you destroy the flavour of your tea by putting sugar in it? It would be equally reasonable to put in pepper or salt. Tea is meant to be bitter, just as beer is meant to be bitter. If you sweeten it, you are no longer tasting the tea, you are merely tasting the sugar; you could make a very similar drink by dissolving sugar in plain hot water.

Tea for Health and Tea for Beauty

Tea is not just a refreshing drink; it is actually good for you too. It is no coincidence that we reach for a cup of tea when we want to cheer up, have had a shock, or feeling a little under the weather.

Health

Studies released in 2011 reveal that black tea, and its components, has been associated with the potential to reduce the risk of cancer, drinking black tea improves cognitive function, and black tea polyphenols prevented weight gain following a high-fat diet. Tea also contains the amino acid, theanine, which is attributed to being the 'pick-me-up' in a cup of tea.

Also in tea are: amino acids; vitamins C, E and K; flavonoids to boost the immune system. Tea provides 17% of your recommended daily allowance of calcium, 22% of vitamin B2 and 5% of zinc, folic acid, vitamins B1 and B6.

Beauty

For shiny hair: steep two tea bags in boiling water for 10 minutes then leave to cool. Rub the cool tea into freshly washed, damp hair. Leave for 10 minutes and rinse. Result – soft, shiny hair.

Brighter Skin: mix a grated potato, a tablespoon of loose black tea with a little olive oil. Massage into your face and rinse in lukewarm water. Result – a natural glow.

Puffy tired or itchy eyes: chill a couple of used tea bags in the fridge. Lay the cold bags over your eyes for 5 – 10 minutes. Result – the puffiness is gone.

Sunburn: laying wet, used tea bags on the affected area takes the sting away, or add 3 or 4 tea bags to your bath and soak for 20 minutes.

Recipes Using Tea

Camomile Tea Mussels with Fennel and White Wine

This recipe is a very fresh and fragrant way to eat mussels, ideal with a crisp glass of wine and some bread for dipping and comes from Stephanie Moon, consultant chef at Rudding Park, Harrogate.

Serves 4

> 2 tbsp of Wharfe Valley or other good quality cold-pressed rapeseed oil
> 3 cloves of garlic peeled and crushed
> 3 large shallots peeled and chopped finely
> 1 large head of fennel, very finely sliced, plus keep the fennel tops for decoration
> 6 good-quality camomile tea bags, or crushed camomile flowers
> 1 ¼ kg mussels, cleaned, washed and scrubbed
> 200 ml of dry white wine (Sauvignon Blanc recommended)

Heat the oil in a high-sided pan.

Add the garlic, shallots and fennel, cover with a lid and cook the vegetables until softened but not browned, 1 – 2 minutes.

Open the tea bags, if the tea bag contains flower heads, tip the flower heads into a pestle and mortar and crush until powdery or finely chop either by hand or in a blender.

Add the tea or crushed camomile flowers and the mussels to the pan.

Add the white wine and then cover the pan with a tight-fitting lid.

Cook on a high heat until all the mussels open, shaking the pan often.

Remove mussels with a slotted spoon and place in a bowl for serving with some of the delicious camomile juices. Decorate with the fennel fronds and serve.

Hot Jasmine-Tea-Smoked Whitby Mackerel

An innovative and delicious way to serve healthy, fresh mackerel, from consultant chef Stephanie Moon at Rudding Park Hotel, Harrogate.

Serves 4
> 250g dried, mixed pulses
> 1 bay leaf
> Salt

For the pickled vegetables:
5 tbsp Womersley Lemon, Basil and Bay vinegar or other fruit vinegars
3 tbsp of caster sugar
Thinly sliced baby carrots and red radish

For the salad dressing:
Zest and juice of 1 lemon
½ tbsp of runny local honey
1 tbsp of Womersley Lemon, Juniper and Bay vinegar or other fruit vinegars
3 tsp of Yorkshire rapeseed oil
Sprigs of your favourite soft leaf herbs

For the mayonnaise:
½ tsp saffron fronds
2 tbsp mayonnaise

For the mackerel:
3 tbsp uncooked rice, any rice will work
2 tbsp of loose Jasmine Tea
2 medium sized mackerel fillets with pin bones removed

Soak the pulses overnight, next day rinse then place into a large pan, cover with cold water, season with a little salt, bay leaf and cook until soft, around 30 mins. Drain and leave to cool.

To pickle the vegetables: simply bring the vinegar and sugar up to the boil, add the thinly sliced vegetables. Cook for 1 minute until softened. Remove from the heat and allow to go cold in the pan. Drain before serving.

To make the dressing for the pulse salad: grate the lemon zest into a bowl, add the honey, lemon juice and vinegar. Whisk in the rapeseed oil and freshly chopped herbs. Check the seasoning.

To make the saffron mayonnaise: simply heat 2 tablespoons of water in a pan with the saffron and once hot, allow to infuse. When cool add the mayonnaise and season if necessary – you can sieve the saffron or if you prefer, leave the tiny flecks of orange saffron in.

Finally to cook the mackerel: heat your smoker and then add the rice mixed with the jasmine tea and place the grid on top. Once smoking, simply place the fillets into the smoker, skin side up, then place directly onto the stove top with the lid tightly on so no smoke escapes and heat again until the fish is cooked (usually around 5 minutes)

Remove the smoker lid.

Dress the cooked pulses with the dressing. Delicately place the fish on the pulse salad, place some pickled baby vegetables on top and fresh herbs to decorate. Spoon the saffron mayonnaise on the edge of the plate and serve.

Enjoy this seasonal summer starter with a crisp glass of iced tea.

Fish, Chips and Tea

This musing on tea with fish and chips comes from renowned chef, Rob Green, from the award-winning Green's Restaurant, Whitby.

No one knows precisely where or when fish and chips came together. Chips (pommes frites) arrived in Britain from France in the 19th century. The first mention in 1854 was when a leading chef included 'thin cut potatoes cooked in oil' in his recipe book, Shilling Cookery. Around this time, fish warehouses sold fried fish and bread, with mention of them in Charles Dickens' novel, *Oliver Twist* published in 1830.

The fish restaurant was introduced into Britain by Samuel Isaacs, who already ran a thriving wholesale fish business throughout London, in the latter part of the 19th century. Isaacs opened his first restaurant in London in 1896 serving fish and chips, bread and butter and tea for nine pence, and its popularity ensured a rapid expansion of the chain.

Take a walk through Whitby town on the East coast of North Yorkshire and every handwritten black board outside every fish and chip shop will show that 100 years later, this is no passing fad.

Serving tea with fish and chips must be one of the oldest drink-food relationships we have in this country. Even people that 'don't drink tea', drink tea with fish and chips.

At Green's we serve our fish & chips in our 'own' newspaper, in a specially designed frying basket, with tartare sauce, lemon and mushy peas. This may sound a bit 'chefy' but it's our tribute to a great British classic.

Green's Fish & Chips Recipe

Serves 2

500g Maris Piper or Arran Victory potatoes (approximately 2 large or 6 small) will make sufficient chips for 2-3 people. It is best to fry in small batches.

2x fillets of cod, haddock or pollock, skinned and boned, dredged in seasoned flour

1 can lager, 250g self-raising flour and 1 tablespoon of malt vinegar whisked together to form a smooth batter the same thickness as double cream. If too thick, the end result will be stodgy.

Lemon, tartare sauce, and mushy peas to serve.

For the fish:

Heat the oil to 190 °C.

Holding the tail of the fish, dip into the batter and make sure all the fish is covered.

Carefully lay the fish into the oil.

Cook until golden brown, turning now and then as soon as the batter has started to crisp.

Depending on the thickness the fish should take between 4 – 6 minutes.

Drain on kitchen paper.

Serve your fish & chips with the lemon, tartare sauce, mushy peas and of course the great British cuppa, Yorkshire Tea for me please!

For the chips:

Peel and chip the potatoes, then wash thoroughly.

Boil large pan of salted water. Add chips and return to boil, then reduce to gentle simmer (no bubbles) for 10 minutes.

Remove chips from water and leave to cool on a cake rack. When cool, chill in fridge.

In a heavy-bottomed saucepan, heat 1.5 litres of groundnut oil to 130°C. Using mesh basket, fry chips for 9 minutes.

Remove basket and shake to remove oil. Cool chips on cake rack, then chill in fridge.

Just before you are ready to eat, heat oil to 190°C. Use mesh basket to fry chips for 2-3 minutes until golden. Cooking times can vary with different hob sizes and potato varieties so keep a close eye on colour of chips. Drain chips, then spread on double layer of kitchen paper.

Black Tea Lentils

The addition of black tea to this vegetarian recipe from Tregothnan Tea in Cornwall adds an extra layer of savoury flavour and a slight smoky quality that is really delicious. Of course, there's no reason why you can't serve this alongside some grilled meat or fish, but it's equally delicious on its own.

960 ml freshly boiled water
4-5 tsp of Tregothnan Classic loose-leaf tea
400g black lentils, rinsed
1 tin of chopped tomatoes
Pinch of Cornish sea salt
Freshly ground black pepper
Fresh herbs, finely chopped (parsley and coriander work really well)

Serves 4 as a side dish, 2 as a main

Steep the black tea leaves in freshly boiled water for 4 minutes until you have a rich liquor, then strain and discard the leaves.

Add the lentils and tomatoes to the tea liquor and bring to the boil over a high heat. Reduce the heat and simmer gently for 30-40 minutes until most of the liquid has evaporated. All the delicious tea flavour will have been absorbed by the lentils, which should be firm, but still tender.

Remove from the heat and allow the lentils to rest in the pan for a further 10 minutes. The rest of the liquid should be absorbed.

Season with a little salt, freshly ground black pepper and a few finely chopped fresh herbs.

Quail with a Jasmine Tea and Prune Sauce

Don't be put off by the deboning of the quail in this recipe, you can buy ready boned from your butcher or some leading supermarkets. If possible, buy Prunes D'Agen or any other plump, soft prunes, not the hard, dry ones.

Serves 6

    250 ml boiling water
    4 heaped tsp Jasmine leaf tea
    175g prunes, finely diced
    6 free range quail
    Salt and black pepper
    2 tbsp olive oil
    2 tbsp unsalted butter
    250 ml chicken stock
    2 tsp clear honey

Pour the boiling water over the tea leaves and leave to soak for 10 minutes or until cool. Mix the tea and diced prunes together and leave to soak for a minimum of 2 hours or as long as overnight. Strain the prunes and press to remove as much liquid as possible. Reserve the juices.

Debone the quail. (If you don't know how to do this ask your butcher to do it for you or buy boneless quail). Season the inside of the quail.

Take 1 heaped tablespoon of the prunes and place over the breast of the quail, sew up the opening. Heat the oil and butter until hot but not burning in a roasting tin on the top of the stove. Roll the quail in the hot oil and butter until coated all over and place in a hot oven, 220°C/450°F/ gas 8, for 20 minutes, turning once during this time.

Remove the quail from the roasting pan and keep warm. Degrease the roasting tin, then deglaze with the prune/tea juices and reduce to a glaze. Finally, deglaze with the chicken stock and reduce by half, then adjust the seasoning, whisk in the honey. Strain through a very fine sieve. Keep warm.

Remove the string from the quail, cut in half lengthways. Serve the two halves on a bed of mashed potatoes (not creamed) and celeriac, a few asparagus tips, and surround with the sauce.

Loose Tea or Bags – You Decide

1. The size of the leaf in loose tea is generally larger than the loose tea leaf in a tea bag; whereas the loose tea in a generic supermarket brand tea bag is generally smaller or broken leaves and can often also be a low-grade tea. When loose tea leaves become broken or crushed the essential oils in the leaf, which give the flavour to tea, are destroyed.

2. Using loose leaf, the loose tea can circulate through the boiling water and swell which means the maximum flavour and colour can be extracted from the leaves. A good-quality tea bag will be more roomy than a cheaper one, so, if you use bags always buy the best quality you can for a better cup of tea.

3. There are some advantages to tea bags; the main being the convenience. Tea bags create no mess or soggy, left over loose tea leaves, so it's quick and easy to clean the tea pot.

Tea-Smoked Duck Breast

Orientally-inspired recipes naturally lend themselves to the addition of fresh or dried tea leaves, and this new twist on a classic duck recipe from Tregothnan Tea in Cornwall is proof. If you're not yet converted to the idea of using tea in your cooking, then this dish is guaranteed to convince you. Use Tregothnan Classic Blend tea, but try experimenting with Green Tea, or even Earl Grey. You'll be surprised how easy it is to smoke your own meat at home, so why not experiment with chicken or fish?

Serves 4

For the duck breasts:
4 duck breasts, skin on
1 tbsp Cornish sea salt
4 tablespoons of vodka

For the marinade:
1 cinnamon stick
10 black peppercorns
3 star anise
1 litre of water
1 tbsp clear honey
1 tbsp of sherry or Chinese rice wine

Juice of 2 limes
1 tbsp Szechuan peppercorns

For the smoking:
4 tbsp Tregothnan loose-leaf Classic blend tea
4 tbsp caster sugar
4 tbsp uncooked rice
3 star anise

Preheat the oven to 200°C/400° F/Gas 6.

Rub the salt all over the duck breasts and skin.

Combine all the marinade ingredients in a large pan or wok, bring to the boil over a high heat and simmer for 10 minutes (which burns off all the alcohol) to bring out the flavours.

Prick the skin of the duck all over with the tip of a sharp knife.

Rinse the duck breasts in fresh water, pat dry, and then re-apply salt. This process will ensure you get nice, crispy skin.

Turn the heat off on the marinade, and place the duck breasts into the mix. Make sure the breasts are coated all over, especially on the skins. This will blanche the duck meat, but not cook it.

Baste them for 2 minutes.

To smoke the meat, line a large roasting tin with foil.

Mix together the dry smoking ingredients and sprinkle evenly over the foil.

Place a cooling rack on top of the mixture and put the duck breasts onto the rack, skin facing down. The meat should not be touching the dry mixture.

Place the roasting tin directly onto your hob and turn the heat up high for a couple of minutes, until the sugar starts to bubble.

Turn the heat down very low, and make a tightly sealed lid for the roasting tray using 2 layers of foil to ensure the smoke doesn't escape.

Leave on the very low heat for a further 10 minutes, then turn off the heat and leave for a further 15 minutes. Do not be tempted to remove the foil in this time!

Remove the duck breasts from the smoker, rub a little vodka into the skin, then pat it dry with a clean tea towel.

To finish cooking the duck, place them skin side up on a clean roasting tray and place in the oven for about 8 minutes.

Remove and leave to rest for 5 minutes before carving and serving.

This is delicious served with noodles, stir fried vegetables, or even a crisp green salad.

Sticky Toffee Pudding with Tea

This tea-soaked pudding dish comes from my former head chef, Peter King of Helmsley. Peter's Sticky Toffee Pudding was one of our best selling puddings.

Adding tea to a classic Sticky Toffee Pudding gives the pudding even more depth. It is a fun recipe as you make it to your taste with more or less tea. According to Peter the pudding is pretty easy to make, don't worry, just enjoy.

Serves 6

For the cake:
300 ml water
200g dried dates
2 strong tea bags
½ tsp bicarbonate of soda
200g soft dark brown sugar
125g butter or margarine
2 eggs, beaten
200g self-raising flour
125 ml condensed milk

For the sauce:
125g soft dark brown sugar
125 ml double cream
125g butter

Heat the oven to 180°C/375°F/Gas 4

Make the cake:

Put the dates in a pan with the water and add the tea bags. Bring to the boil to soften the dates. Add the bicarbonate of soda, stir to dissolve, then remove the tea bags.

In a bowl, add the sugar, butter or margarine and beat with a mixer until creamed together and fluffy. Add the eggs and beat again.

Fold in the flour, followed by the date mixture.

Add the condensed milk (adding condensed milk makes the pudding more dense and sticky – leave out if a firmer pudding is

required).

Line a 22 x 30 cm cake tin with greaseproof paper and pour the mixture in.

Bake for 40 minutes or until firm and there is no raw cake mixture when pricked with a knife.

Make the sauce:

Place all the ingredients in a pan and bring to the boil and simmer until golden brown.

When cooked you can either pour the sauce on the pudding while warm so it soaks into it and then serve or cut the pudding into squares then warm later and pour gently warmed sauce over it.

Serve with ice-cream on the top.

Green Tea Ice Cream

If you don't want to drink green tea in the cup, another way to enjoy the reviving tea is in a rich ice cream. The ice cream is best made in an ice cream maker, but don't worry if you don't have one, just follow the instructions below.

Serves 4

> 250 ml full fat milk
> 150g granulated sugar
> Tiny pinch of salt
> 500 ml double cream
> 4 tsp green tea powder
> 6 large free-range egg yolks

In a medium-sized saucepan, gently warm the milk with the sugar and salt until all the sugar has dissolved.

Place the cream into a large bowl, add the tea powder and whisk until all the powder is incorporated.

In another bowl beat the eggs then slowly pour in the warmed milk mixture (not hot - you don't want to create scrambled eggs) whisking constantly. Return the mixture to the pan and whilst stirring, warm through until the mixture is thick enough to coat the back of the spoon.

Remove from the heat and strain into the double cream and whisk the two together thoroughly. Cool the mixture over a bowl of ice cubes until cooled – whisk from time to time to prevent a skin forming.

Once the cream is completely cold either churn in an ice cream maker or place the mixture into a plastic box and pop it in the freezer. Every hour remove the box and beat thoroughly to break up any ice crystals. Repeat until the ice cream is smooth and frozen.

Mrs Beeton's Tea Cream Recipe

This simple tea cream recipe comes from *Mrs Beeton's Book of Household Management*, the 19th century weighty tome of recipes and advice for the housewife. The recipe may be centuries old but is still good today.

Serves 4

½ pint milk
1 oz of good tea
½ pint of double cream
⅔ oz of gelatine
Sugar to taste

Bring the milk to boiling point, pour it over the tea and let it infuse for 20 minutes, then strain and add half the cream.

Dissolve the gelatine in a little boiling water, strain it into the cream and sweeten to taste.

Whip the remainder of the cream stiffly, stir it into the tea when sufficiently cool.

Pour into a mould rinsed with cold water and leave it to set.

Time – about 1 hour

Average Cost – 2s

Sufficient for 4 or 5 persons

"Some people will tell you there is a great deal of poetry and fine sentiment in a chest of tea."
Ralph Waldo Emerson, *Letters and Social Aims*

Masala Chai Recipe

The word chai on its own is simply the word for tea, but for the English, the term is synonymous with Masala Chai, the spiced black tea from India. A strong Assam tea makes a good base for the tea as it can easily hold its own with the spices. The tea was traditionally sweetened with jaggery, a form of unrefined cane sugar, but more often is served with ordinary sugar and will normally be served with whole milk. The blend of spices can change from family to family but will generally be a blend of the 'warm' spices such as cardamom, cinnamon and pepper. Care should be taken with the cloves so as not to overpower the Masala Chai.

450 ml water
3 whole cloves
½ stick cinnamon
4 cardamom pods
4 black peppercorns

225 ml whole milk
3 tsp black tea, Assam or a good English Breakfast tea leaves
Sugar to taste

Heat the hot water in a pan.

Place all the spices in a pestle and mortar and crush very, very lightly to just bruise the spices, not break them and add to the hot water.

Simmer gently for 6 – 8 minutes (do not boil the spices).

Add the milk, stir and simmer again for 1 minute.

Remove the pan from the heat, add the tea leaves and steep for 3 minutes.

Strain into cups and serve.

"I say let the world go to hell, but I should always have my tea."
Fyodor Dostoyevsky, *Notes from Underground*

Masala Chai

Earl Grey Drizzle Cake

Earl Grey Tea is a very popular ingredient when cooking with tea as the flavour of Bergamot in the tea adds a distinctive, yet delicate flavour. It is especially lovely when used in cakes and buns.

300ml boiling water
2 Earl Grey tea bags
5 tbsp milk
175g unsalted butter, softened

175g caster sugar
3 large free-range eggs
225g self raising flour
200g icing sugar

Preheat the oven to 180°C/365°F/Gas.

Grease a 22cm sandwich tin with butter and line with baking paper.

Put the boiling water in a measuring jug and add 1 of the teabags, leave to brew for 5 minutes and then remove the teabag, set the jug aside for the tea to cool completely.

In a small pan, add the second teabag and the milk and on a very low heat infuse, stirring for 2-3 minutes not letting the milk boil. Remove from the heat and set aside to cool.

With an electric whisk set on medium, cream the butter and sugar together until very pale and fluffy.

Add the eggs one at a time whisking thoroughly after each addition.

Add the infused milk and continue to whisk.

Add the flour to the mixture and gently fold in using a metal spoon.

Pour the mixture into the prepared tin and bake in the oven for 45-50 minutes until a skewer inserted into the middle comes out clean.

Take out of the oven and leave to cool for 10 minutes in the tin and then turn out onto a wire rack to cool completely.

When the cake is completely cooled use a skewer to make holes all over the cake.

Sieve the icing sugar into a large mixing bowl and add 2 tbsp of the ready made Earl Grey tea, stir thoroughly. The consistency should run slowly off the back of a wooden spoon. Discard any left over tea once you have the correct consistency.

Pour the syrup into the centre of the cake letting it slowly drizzle through the holes and spreading evenly over the cake. Leave the cake until the syrup starts to crust and serve.

"Take some more tea," the March Hare said to Alice, very earnestly.
"I've had nothing yet," Alice replied in an offended tone, "so I can't take more."
"You mean you can't take less," said the Hatter: "it's very easy to take more than nothing."
"Nobody asked your opinion," said Alice."
Lewis Carroll, *Alice in Wonderland*

Shirley's Tea

A delightfully refreshing non-alcoholic drink from Claire Trumper, owner of Trumpers Tea in rural Herefordshire. Claire has over 20 years' experience in the tea industry as a consultant and tea aficionado. She has spent many years abroad in tea plantations helping build communities and commerce. She has now developed her own blends of fairly traded teas and consults on environmental projects overseas. Trumpers Tea can be bought on-line at www.trumperstea.co.uk

1 part Darjeeling tea   Maraschino cherries
1 part ginger ale   Slice of orange
Splash of Grenadine

Pour equal measures of cooled Darjeeling tea and ginger ale into a glass with ice.

Add a splash of Grenadine and garnish with a maraschino cherry or two and a slice of orange.

Iced Tea

Iced tea is not as popular in Britain as it is in other countries, particularly the United States, even though it is a refreshing drink and a great way to enjoy tea on a hot summer's day. From using straightforward black tea, infusions and tea blends, to adding favourite flavours both fruit and spicy, the recipes for iced tea are endless. This is a basic recipe for iced black tea, add to it any flavours you wish to ring the changes.

6 tsp loose black tea   1 pint boiling water   Ice cubes

Steep the black tea with the boiling water for 5 mins. If using spices or ginger steep these with the tea.

Strain the tea into a large jug two-thirds filled with ice cubes.

Recipes for Afternoon Tea

The delights of a traditional Afternoon Tea involve the eating of not only savoury finger-sized sandwiches, but lovely scones, tarts, buns, tray bakes and cakes. Here's a selection of traditional and more modern, and innovative recipes to enjoy.

Scones for Afternoon Tea

Home-made scones for afternoon tea are either, sweet or savoury, delicious hot or cold and an intrinsic part of afternoon tea. The success of scones depends on working as quickly as possible, keeping all the ingredients cool.

Makes 6 – 8 scones

225g self-raising flour
55g cold butter
1 level tsp baking powder
½ tsp salt

150 ml milk
1 egg beaten with a little milk

Heat the oven to 200°C/400°F/Gas 6

Grease and flour a baking sheet. Sieve the flour into a roomy baking bowl, add the butter, baking powder and salt. Rub the butter into the flour until the mixture resembles fine breadcrumbs. Make a well in the centre and using a dinner knife, stir in enough milk to make a soft, pliable dough.

Turn the mixture on to a floured board and knead very lightly until just smooth, then lightly roll out to 2cm thick. Cut rounds with a 7.5cm cutter or cut into triangles with a sharp knife.

Place on the baking tray and brush with the beaten egg and milk mixture. Bake near the top of the hot oven for 15 minutes or until golden brown and well risen. Cool on a wire rack before eating. Serve with butter, or lashings of jam and cream.

For Fruit Scones: add 50g sultanas or chopped dates to the dry ingredients in the basic recipe.

For Cheese Scones: 50g grated cheese and 1/2 tsp dry mustard powder to the mixture after rubbing in the fat and flour and continue with the basic recipe. Sprinkle the scones with 50g more grated cheese before baking the scones in the oven.

Tea Cup Cheesecake

A brilliant recipe from my stepdaughter Lucy. Cheesecake is elevated to another league in this, a novel and charming way of serving it, in a vintage tea cup.

For the base:
10 digestive biscuits
75g butter, melted
1 tbsp honey

For the filling:
335g soft cream cheese
180g caster sugar
210 ml double cream
Juice and zest of 1 lemon
1-2 punnets raspberries

Serves 4 – 6 (depending on size of cups)

Roughly crush the biscuits and stir into the melted butter combining thoroughly. Add the honey and stir again. Once combined, add about 2 tbsp of the crumbs into the tea cups and gently press down to create a level surface, cover the biscuit base with a handful of raspberries.

In a large bowl beat the soft cheese and sugar together. In a separate bowl whip the cream until very thick, fold the cream and the soft cheese together. Add the lemon juice and zest and fold thoroughly until you are left with a smooth even mixture.

Carefully spoon the mixture on top of the raspberries and use the back of the spoon to smooth the top, refrigerate for at least 3 hrs before serving but overnight is best. Decorate with a handful of raspberries.

Tea Cup Cheese Cake

Lucy's Chocolate Macaroons

Lucy's Chocolate Macaroons

Macaroons are not the easiest to make. However, my stepdaughter Lucy has cracked the method with her lovely recipe for chocolate macaroons. She uses a silicone macaroon mat from www.lakeland.co.uk, which creates a perfect shape every time.

For the macaroons:
130g icing sugar
1 tbsp cocoa powder
100g almonds, ground
2 medium free-range egg whites

For the filling:
50g milk chocolate
2 tsp slightly warmed milk

Preheat the oven to 180°C/365°F/Gas 4.

Sieve the icing sugar and cocoa powder into a large mixing bowl and slowly combine with the ground almonds. In a separate bowl whisk the egg whites until they form peaks, then carefully fold into the other ingredients.

Fill a piping bag with the mixture (make sure the almonds have been well ground as large lumps can get blocked in smaller nozzles), pipe small blobs onto the silicone sheet laid flat on a work surface. Less is more at this stage as the mixture will settle and form into the allotted spaces. Leave the mixture to dry for at least 10 minutes.

Bake for 15-20 minutes until they feel firm and come away from the silicone sheet easily. Cool completely on the sheet while you make the filling.

Break the chocolate into small pieces and add to a heatproof bowl over a pan of lightly simmering water. When melted add the milk and stir until the mixture becomes smooth and easily spreadable.

Place roughly 1/2 a tsp of the filling to the flat side of one macaroon and sandwich together with another, twist together gently. Continue with the remaining macaroons and serve.

Nana Marshall's Flapjack

I make a pretty good flapjack, but, according to my stepchildren, their Nana Marshall makes the best. Having tried it, I have to agree.

115g margarine	65g coconut
115g soft brown sugar	95g rolled oats
1 tbsp golden syrup	1 tsp bicarbonate of soda
115g plain flour	

Preheat the oven to 180°C/375°F/Gas 4

Grease a 22cm baking tin with butter.

In a large mixing bowl thoroughly combine all the ingredients together using your hand.

Press the mixture gently into the prepared tin and cook for 20 minutes.

Remove from the oven and leave to cool completely in the tin.

Cut when cooled and serve.

Note: You can change the flavours of the flapjack by removing the coconut and replacing with dried apricots, mixed dried fruit or dates.

"When you have nobody you can make a cup of tea for, when nobody needs you, that's when I think life is over."
Audrey Hepburn

Lucy's Mini Victoria Sponge Cakes

These mini sponges are based on a classic Victoria sponge but made using a mini sponge cake tin from www.lakeland.co.uk. This unique way of serving the delicious little cakes comes from my stepdaughter Lucy, who is both a creative and talented baker.

Makes 12

170g very soft unsalted butter
170g caster sugar
½ tsp vanilla extract
3 free-range eggs

170g self-raising flour
2 tbsp strawberry jam
12 large fresh strawberries
100 ml double cream
Icing sugar for dusting

Preheat the oven 160°C/325°F/ Gas 3

Butter and line the insides of 12 mini Victoria sandwich tins.

In a mixing bowl, beat together the butter and caster sugar until pale and fluffy.

Add the vanilla extract and one egg, beat well and add 1 tbsp of the flour. Once combined add a second egg beating well and adding an additional tbsp of flour. Finally add the third egg beat well, add the remaining flour and mix well.

Divide the mixture in to the 12 tins filling the individual sections about ½ full.

Bake in the oven for 20 minutes or until a skewer inserted in the middle comes out clean.

Cool the cakes in the tin for about 10 minutes and turn out on to a wire rack until completely cooled.

Whip the cream to very soft peaks just stiff enough that they can hold their own shape. Add the 2 tbsp of jam and fold in gently until combined. Fill a silicone piping bag with large nozzle with the cream.

With an apple corer gently twist into the centre of each individual cake and pull out, the cake should resemble a very fluffy tall doughnut.

Insert the nozzle of the piping bag into the hole and fill, when the cream has reached the top slowly pull the piping bag out so you get a delicious dollop of cream on top of the cake.

Once all the cakes are filled cut the top off each strawberry and cut into three, fan the strawberries on top of the dollop of cream and dust lightly with icing sugar.

Bakewell Tart

Bakewell tart is the famous British tart made in the picturesque town of Bakewell in the Derbyshire Peak District. The almondy tart is perfect for an Afternoon Tea as it is not too heavy but packed with flavour.

For the pastry:
150g plain flour
Pinch of salt
80g butter, cubed or an equal mix of butter and lard
2-3 tbsp cold water
1 egg white, lightly beaten

For the filling:
2 tbsp raspberry jam
150g butter
150g caster sugar
3 medium eggs plus 1 yolk, beaten
150g ground almonds
Zest of 1 medium lemon
2 tbsp flaked almonds

Make the pastry:

Heat the oven 170°C/350°F/Gas 3

Place the flour, butter and salt into a large clean bowl.

Rub the butter into the flour with your fingertips until the mixture resembles fine breadcrumbs, working as quickly as possible to prevent the dough becoming warm.

Add the water to the mixture and using a cold knife stir until the dough binds together, add more cold water, a teaspoon at a time, if the mixture is too dry.

Wrap the dough in cling film and chill for a minimum of 15 minutes, up to 30 minutes.

Make the tart:

Roll out the pastry on a lightly floured board to 5mm thick. Grease and then line a 20cm deep tart tin with the pastry. Prick the base all over with a fork. Chill in the refrigerator for 15 minutes.

Line the tart case with baking/greaseproof paper and fill with baking beans. Cook for 15 minutes or until the pastry is a pale golden colour. Remove the baking beans, lightly brush the inside of the pastry case with a little egg white, cook for a further 5 minutes. Spread the raspberry jam onto the base of the pastry case. Leave to cool.

Cream the butter and sugar together until pale in colour using an electric hand whisk. Add the beaten eggs and egg yolk a little at a time. Gently fold in the ground almonds and lemon zest.

Pour the mixture in to the pastry case and gently level the surface to ensure the whole case is filled. Bake for 20 minutes. Sprinkle the flaked almonds on to the surface and bake for a further 20 minutes or until golden and set.

Leave to cool and serve with custard sauce or cream.

The tart can also be made as individual portions. Use a 12-hole bun tin instead of a tart tin and follow the methods as above.

"The British have an umbilical cord which has never been cut and through which tea flows constantly. It is curious to watch them in times of sudden horror, tragedy or disaster. The pulse stops apparently and nothing can be done, and no move made, until "a nice cup of tea" is quickly made. There is no question that it brings solace and does steady the mind."
Marlene Dietrich

Prize-Winning Dairy Free Cup Cakes

These delightful cup cakes come from Tracey Wrigglesworth, winner of the Boroughbridge Show Baking Competition. These, however, are not just any cakes. Tracey loves to bake for her granddaughters, Jessie Mae and Lillia Grace Mulholland, but unfortunately one is dairy intolerant. So, Tracey set about devising a recipe for her dietary needs which looked and tasted wonderful. No wonder the judges were impressed.

225g dairy-free margarine	225g sponge flour or good
225g caster sugar	quality self-raising flour
4 medium free-range eggs	1 tsp vanilla extract

Preheat the oven to 180°C/375°F/Gas 4

Using an electric hand whisk, cream the sugar and margarine until light and fluffy. Beat in the eggs one at a time with a little flour.

Carefully fold the remaining flour in until fully incorporated then fold in the vanilla extract.

Place the mixture into the cup cake cases filling almost to the top and bake in the oven for 25 minutes, until well risen and golden brown. Leave to cool on a wire cooling rack and decorate.

Cream Topping: whisk dairy-free margarine with icing sugar. Decorate with Jelly Tots, marshmallows and/or fresh strawberries with a sprinkling of 80% cocoa chocolate.

Classic Victoria Sponge Cake

A Classic Victoria Sponge Cake

A classic Victoria Sponge is right at the top of the list of baking delights. The delicate sponge filled with jam and cream is the stuff of village fetes and the WI, and fierce competition abounds for who can create the lightest, softest sponge. A secret though, it's not that difficult, just check out the tips below and follow the quick and easy recipe and you are on to a winner.

3 large free-range eggs	A jar of quality strawberry
225g caster sugar	jam
225g self-raising flour	200 ml whipping cream,
2 tsp baking powder	whipped to firm peaks
125g softened butter	Icing sugar and fresh
100g margarine	strawberries to decorate

Preheat the oven to 180°C/350°F/Gas 4.

Lightly grease 2 x 20cm sandwich tins with butter. Line the bottom with greased baking paper.

Using an electric mixer, mix together the eggs, sugar, flour and baking powder plus the butter and margarine until combined. The resulting mixture should be a soft, dropping consistency. If you don't have an electric mixer use a wooden spoon.

Divide the mixture evenly between the two cake tins and smooth the surface of the cake. Pop both cakes onto the middle shelf of the preheated oven. Cook for 25 minutes or until the cakes are well risen and golden brown on the surface. If the cakes are browning too quickly lower the temperature just slightly but do not be tempted to open the door.

Once they are risen and brown you can open the door to check, by gently pressing the centre of the cake it should spring back easily. Remove the cakes from the oven and place on a cooling rack for 5 minutes. After the 5 minutes the cakes should be shrinking away from the sides of the cake tins. Carefully remove the cakes from the tins and leave to cool completely on the cooling rack.

Once cooled, place one cake cooked side down onto a plate. Cover with a thick layer of strawberry jam followed by an even thicker layer of whipped cream. Top with the second cake. Dredge with the icing sugar, and decorate with fresh strawberries if you wish. Serve with a nice cup of tea.

A few tips for the perfect Victoria Sponge

- Before you begin any mixing, weigh out all the ingredients. Line the tin and preheat the oven so when you come to start mixing you will be able to work as quickly and smoothly as possible which creates a light cake.

- Make sure your ingredients are at room temperature; cold eggs do not whip up easily or hold the same volume of air; cold butter is hard to whisk in. Any of these will result in a hard, heavy cake.

- Always use the freshest eggs possible. The white of fresh eggs will whip up into a frenzy of air, whereas older eggs struggle to hold it together.

- Always mix the baking powder with the flour and then sift. Sifting adds air and thus lightness to a cake mixture. Use a cake flour if available, as cake flour tends to be finer milled.

- Do not be tempted to open the oven door until the cakes are almost cooked.

Welsh Cakes

These little cakes are cooked on a bakestone or maen, that is the stone on which they are griddled. Although bakestones are found in all the Celtic countries, only in Wales do we griddle these sweet cakes. A heavy frying pan works well, but take care not to let the sugar in your Welsh cakes burn.

This recipe comes from Gilli Davies. Gilli is the author of the renowned book of Welsh food, Flavours of Wales, *published by Graffeg, which was nominated for a Gourmand World Book Award in 2012.*

100g mixed butter and lard	75g currants
225g self-raising flour	½ tsp mixed spice
Pinch of salt	1 tsp honey
75g caster sugar	1 medium egg, beaten

In a bowl, rub the fats into the flour and salt until the mixture resembles breadcrumbs.

Stir in the sugar, currants, mixed spice and honey.

Add the beaten egg and mix to form a firm dough.

On a floured board, roll or pat the mixture until about 2cm thick.

Cut into 6cm discs and griddle over a medium heat until golden brown on both sides.

Dust the Welsh cakes with caster sugar and eat immediately or store in an airtight tin.

"I am in no way interested in immortality, but only in the taste of tea."
Lu T'ung

Yorkshire Curd Tart

Yorkshire Curd Tart is a specialty tart from the beautiful county of Yorkshire and created as a way to use up left over fresh curd from the cheese making process.

Fresh curds can be bought from a dairy, but otherwise are difficult to get hold of. However, making your own is easy but you will need to start the day before you make the tart.

Serves 8

For the curds:
1 litre full cream milk
2 tbsp rennet

For the pastry:
125g plain flour
Pinch of salt
55g butter, cubed or an equal mix of butter and lard
2 - 3 tbsp cold water

For the filling:
100g unsalted butter, softened
50g fine caster sugar
2 medium free-range eggs, well beaten
Pinch salt
¼ tsp freshly grated nutmeg
¼ tsp ground allspice
1 rounded tbsp fresh white breadcrumbs
50g plump, seedless raisins
50g currants

Make the curds:

Place the milk into a saucepan and over a gentle heat. Bring to blood temperature (37°C/98°F). Remove from the heat, stir in the rennet and leave in a cool place (not the fridge) to set. Once cooled and set, gently break up the mixture into large chunks, using a fork.

Line a large sieve or colander with fine muslin or cheesecloth and place over a large bowl. Spoon the chunks of curd into the sieve or colander and leave to drain for at least 6 hours, preferably overnight.

Make the pastry:

Heat the oven 170°C/325°F/Gas 3

Place the flour, butter and salt into a large clean bowl. Rub the butter into the flour with your fingertips until the mixture resembles fine breadcrumbs. Add the water to the mixture and using a cold knife, stir until the dough binds together. Wrap the dough in cling film and chill for 30 minutes.

Make the tart:

Roll out the pastry to 5mm thick. Grease and line a 4cm deep x 20cm tart tin, with the pastry. Prick the base all over with a fork. Chill in the refrigerator for 15 mins.

Line the pastry case with baking paper and fill with baking beans. Cook for 15 minutes or until the pastry is a pale golden colour. Remove the paper and beans and leave to cool.

In a large baking bowl, cream the butter and sugar together until fluffy and light and pale in colour. Tip the curd mixture from the sieve/colander into the creamed butter. Add the beaten eggs, salt, nutmeg, allspice and beat well until all the ingredients are well incorporated. Finally stir in the breadcrumbs, raisins and currants. Pour the curd mixture into the prepared tart case and bake in the oven for 30 minutes until golden brown. Leave the tart to cool, then serve.

Yorkshire Curd Tart is best eaten slightly warm. Always eat the tart within 24 hours of making.

"You can never get a cup of tea large enough or a book long enough to suit me."
C.S. Lewis

Zingy Tuscan Lemon Tart

I was taught how to make this zingy lemon tart in Tuscany and every time I make it, it is like bringing a little Tuscan sun into the kitchen.

Don't be put off by the amount of eggs and lemon in the recipe - it is so rich and flavourful, a small piece goes a long way.

Serves 8

225g plain flour
2 tbsp sugar
Pinch salt
110g cold butter, diced
2 tbsp cold water

For the filling:
Grated zest and juice of 7 lemons
350g caster sugar
6 whole free-range eggs
9 egg yolks
300g unsalted butter, softened

Heat the oven to 190°C/375°F/Gas 5

Make the pastry:

Place the flour, sugar, salt and butter into the bowl of a food processor.

Using only the pulse setting, pulse until the mixture resembles breadcrumbs. Avoid over mixing if you can.

Through the funnel on the top of the processor, slowly add the water a little at a time until the mixture comes together in a ball. Add more water, a teaspoon at a time, if the mixture doesn't stick together and pulse again.

Wrap the pastry in cling film and chill in the refrigerator for 30 minutes.

Butter a 25cm loose-bottomed tart tin.

Unwrap the pastry, roll and line the tart dish making sure it is even on the bottom and sides and there are no holes. Prick the base of the dish using a fork. Refrigerate again for 15 minutes.

Cover the pastry with baking parchment and fill with baking beans, or use long grain rice. Bake for 25 minutes in the preheated oven, remove the parchment and beans or rice and bake for a further 10 minutes until the crust is golden.

Leave until completely cold.

Meanwhile make the filling:

Place the lemon zest, juice, sugar, eggs and egg yolks into a large roomy saucepan.

Over a very low heat, whisk to incorporate all the ingredients and continue to whisk until the sugar has dissolved. Take your time with this process, do not be tempted to turn the heat up or you will scramble the eggs. Slowly, the mixture will begin to thicken and is ready when thick enough to coat the back of a wooden spoon.

Remove the pan from the heat and place on a cold surface. Continue to whisk for 5 minutes to cool the mixture down. Once cool, whisk in the softened butter.

Raise the oven temperature to 230°C/450°F/Gas 8.

Pour the mixture into the pastry base. Place near the top of the hot oven and bake until the top is brown, about 8 minutes. You can also brown the surface using a chef's blowtorch if you have one but take care not to burn the surface.

Serve at room temperature.

Shortbread Recipe

A quick and irresistibly delicious Scottish shortbread recipe. The success of a 'shortie', as shortbread is also known, is to handle the dough with care. Do not pound or knead heavily, and make sure your hands and the dishes you use are cold. The resulting shortbread will then be light and crumbly with a dense buttery taste.

225g butter
Tiny pinch of salt
110g caster sugar, plus extra for sprinkling
225g plain flour, plus extra for dusting
100g cornflour

Preheat the oven to 170°C/325°F/Gas 3.

In a large bowl cream together the butter, salt and sugar until light and fluffy and pale in colour. This can take at least 10 minutes. Alternatively use a food mixer.

Mix together the flour and cornflour and sieve into the bowl of butter and sugar. Mix quickly and thoroughly to bring all the ingredients together but do not over mix.

Tip the mixture onto a lightly floured work surface and knead lightly and quickly to form a loose dough.

Then either:

Roll out the dough between 2 sheets of parchment paper to 1 cm thick.

Prick the surface all over with a fork.

Cut into desired shape or rounds using cookie cutters.

Place the Scottish shortbreads on a lightly greased baking sheet and bake for 25 minutes or until pale brown and crisp.

Sprinkle the warm Scottish shortbreads with caster sugar and leave to cool on a wire cooling rack.

Or:

Grease a Swiss roll tin 23 x 33cm with butter.

Press the dough into the tin and press with your fingers to level the surface, prick all over with a fork.

Bake in the preheated oven for 45 minutes or until golden brown.

With the shortbread still in the tin, cut into squares or fingers.

Leave to cool for 15 minutes then carefully remove to a wire cooling rack.

Store in an airtight tin or box.

"Drink your tea slowly and reverently, as if it is the axis on which the world earth revolves - slowly, evenly, without rushing toward the future."
Thich Nhat Hanh

Kath's Chocolate Cake Recipe

This chocolate cake recipe is voted one of the best chocolate cakes ever by my friends and family. Kathleen's chocolate cake is the chocolate cake recipe from Kathleen Grant, the mother of one of my oldest friends. Sadly Kathleen died several years ago and her recipe book, written over a number of years, was found when sorting through her belongings.

Kathleen uses margarine in the recipe; it was written at a time when margarine was preferable to butter which was in short supply after WWII. I recommend you now use a mixture of soft butter and margarine, it works even better and adds much more flavour to the cake.

175g sugar	1 ½ tsp baking powder
175g of either margarine or half margarine and half softened butter	140g self-raising flour
	40g cocoa
	2 tbsp warm milk
3 large free-range eggs, beaten	2 tbsp boiling water

Preheat the oven to 180°C/350°F/Gas 4

In a large baking bowl cream the sugar with the margarine and butter until light and fluffy and very pale in colour. You can use either an electric hand whisk, wooden spoon, or fork.

Add the beaten egg a little at a time and beat well.

Sieve the cocoa with the flour and baking powder. Fold gently into the butter and egg mixture. Finally, add the milk and boiling water, stir well.

Grease 2 x 18cm cake tins. Divide the mixture between the two tins and gently spread to create a smooth surface.

Bake in the preheated oven for 20 - 25 minutes until risen. To check the cake is cooked insert a metal skewer into the centre, it should come out clean with crumbs on it, not cake mixture.

Remove the cakes from the tins and leave to cool on a wire rack. Once cooled decorate as desired.

You can fill the cake with jam, jam and cream or a chocolate icing. The spreadable icing can also be used on the top of the cake.

To make spreadable icing:

Melt 150ml of double cream and 150g dark, plain chocolate, broken into pieces in a large heatproof basin placed over a pan of simmering water. Once melted, stir thoroughly then leave to cool and thicken.

Battenberg Cake

Battenberg Cake is believed to have been named in honour of the marriage of Queen Victoria's granddaughter to Prince Louis of Battenberg in 1884. No cake is more frivolous, and at any Afternoon Tea, in fact at any occasion, bring out a Battenberg cake and watch smiles all round.

150g butter, softened, plus extra for greasing
150g caster sugar
3 large free-range eggs, beaten
1 tsp vanilla extract
150g self-raising flour

30 ml milk
2 drops of pink food colouring
75g apricot jam, warmed with 2 drops of water
200g marzipan, ready rolled

Preheat the oven to 200°C/400°F/Gas 6.

In a large baking bowl beat together the butter and sugar until light and creamy.

Slowly add the beaten eggs, beating constantly. Add the vanilla extract, milk and stir. Sieve the flour into the baking bowl and continue beating until smooth.

Place half of the mixture in another bowl, add the food colouring a little at a time until you have a colour you like and stir well.

Grease a 15cm square cake tin and divide into 2 by placing a thick layer of aluminium foil down the centre. Put the pink mixture into one side and the plain mixture in the other. Place in the oven for 25-30 minutes, or until the cake springs back when pressed lightly. Remove from the oven and leave to cool on a wire rack.

Cut each cake to the same size, then cut each cake in half lengthways. Take a pink cake and brush one side with the warmed jam. Place a yellow piece next to it, jam side together and push gently together. Brush the top surface with jam and place a piece of yellow cake on top of a pink piece and vice versa. Brush all the outside edges with more jam.

Brush the rolled marzipan with a little jam and wrap it all around the cake, hiding the seam underneath. Trim away any excess. Chill the cake in the refrigerator for at least an hour before serving.

Bara Brith

No Welsh Afternoon Tea would be complete without this tea bread, known as Bara Brith or literally – speckled bread. The recipe comes from Gilli Davies. Gilli is the author of the renowned book of Welsh food, Flavours of Wales, published by Graffeg, which was nominated for a Gourmand World Book Award 2012.

450g mixed, dried fruit	2 tbsp soft brown sugar
300 ml cold tea	1 tsp mixed spice
2 tbsp marmalade	450g self-raising flour
1 free-range egg, beaten	Honey to glaze

Soak the fruit overnight in the tea.

Next day, mix in the marmalade, egg, sugar, spice and flour. Spoon into a greased 900g loaf tin and bake in a warm oven 170°C/325°F/Gas 3 for 1 ¾ hours, or until the centre is cooked through.

Check from time to time to see that the top doesn't brown too much, and cover with a sheet of foil if necessary.

Once cooked, leave the Bara Brith to stand for 5 minutes, then remove from the tin and place on a cooling tray, brush honey over the top to glaze.

Dominic's Yorkshire Fruit Tea Cake

This Yorkshire fruit cake recipe comes from Yorkshire sculptor Dominic Hopkinson. Not only is Dominic a talented sculptor, he is an avid foodie and developed this recipe from one his mum used to make.

The success of this deliciously rich, moist cake lies in soaking the dried mixed fruits in strong dark tea the evening before; the tea adds a subtle depth of flavour to the cake. For this reason you will need a little advance planning to allow time to soak the fruits. It is worth it though so don't be put off.

You can use a prepared dried fruit mixture available in most supermarkets, or blend your own to create an individual cake, balance the mixture to your preferences. Be warned though, one slice will never be enough.

450g dried fruit - sultanas, currants, raisins and chopped dates	100 ml brandy or sherry
	½ tsp freshly ground nutmeg
	2 tsp lemon juice
300 ml cold, strong, black tea	1 tsp baking powder
150g butter, slightly softened	110g ground almonds
150g dark Muscovado sugar	225g chopped, mixed candied peel
4 medium free-range eggs	
225g plain flour	225g glace cherries, halved
1 tbsp dark treacle	

The day before place the dried fruits in a large bowl, add the tea and stir well. Cover and leave overnight.

Preheat the oven to 170°C/350°F/Gas 3.

Line a 22cm round cake tin with greaseproof paper or baking parchment.

Place the butter and sugar into a large baking bowl. Using an electric hand whisk or fork, cream the butter into the sugar until light, smooth and creamy.

Beat one egg into the creamed butter, then beat in a quarter of the flour. Repeat until all the eggs and flour are used up.

Add the treacle, brandy or sherry, nutmeg and lemon juice to the cake mixture and stir gently using a spoon or spatula. Finally, stir in the baking powder.

Drain the dried fruits and add the ground almonds, glace cherries and mixed, candied peel. Stir well then add to the cake mixture stirring gently until all the fruits are incorporated into the mixture. Stir gently so as not to 'flatten' the cake mixture.

Spoon the mixture into the prepared cake tin and gently level the surface. Cook in the preheated oven for 2 - 2½ hours or until dark, golden brown.

Leave to cool slightly before removing from the tin, then leave to cool completely on a wire rack. The cake will keep well stored in an airtight tin.

Tea Facts *from the British Tea Council*

160 million... the number of cups of tea drunk every day in Britain.

Tea break time... tea breaks are a tradition that has been with us for approximately 200 years.

Drink your way to the top... 80% of office workers claim they find out more about what's going on at work over a cup of tea than in any other way.

A long time ago... tea was created more than 5000 years ago in China.

The first book... about tea was written by Lu Yu in 800 A.D.

Arrived in Europe... tea firstly appeared in Europe thanks to Portuguese Jesuit Father Jasper de Cruz in 1560.

Everyone's favourite... by the middle of the 18th century tea had replaced ale and gin as the drink of the masses and had become Britain's most popular beverage.

Good for you... tea contains half the amount of caffeine found in coffee.

How many cups a day... the number of recommended cups of tea to drink each day is 4; this gives you optimal benefit.

A cup of tea to keep the dentist away... tea is a natural source of fluoride, which helps protect against tooth decay and gum disease.

And the doctor... tea has potential health maintenance benefits in cardiovascular disease and cancer prevention.

Big in India... apart from tourism, tea production is the biggest industrial activity in India.

Other British and Irish names for a cup of tea			
A cuppa	*Rosie Lee*	*Cuppo the tea*	*Kippertae*
Cup o' char	*A brew*	*Scooby Doo*	*Cup av tay*

As you like it... 98% of people take their tea with milk, but only 30% take it with sugar.

Bag it up... 96% of all cups of tea drunk daily in the UK are brewed from tea bags.

The first tea bag... appeared commercially in 1904 made from hand-sewn silk muslin bags and marketed worldwide by Thomas Sullivan. The heat sealed bags we are more familiar with today came into use around 1930.

Tea Superstitions

Putting milk in tea before sugar is to cross the path of love but never to marry.

Making tea stronger than usual means a new friendship.

Two teaspoons accidentally placed together on the same saucer means a wedding or a pregnancy.

Bubbles in the cup means kisses are coming.

Two women pouring from the same pot, then one will be pregnant within the year.

Undissolved sugar in the bottom of your teacup, someone has a crush on you.

Spilling tea whilst making it is a lucky omen.

Stir the tea anti-clockwise stirs up trouble.

A floating tea leaf, then a stranger is coming.

Accidentally leave the lid off the teapot then expect a stranger bearing ill tidings.

If you are worried about evil spirits bringing trouble to your home scatter dried tea leaves on the doorstep to protect yourself.

"There are few hours in life more agreeable than the hour
dedicated to the ceremony known as afternoon tea."
Henry James, *The Portrait of a Lady*

All Things Tea

Buy Specialist Teas Online

Brew HaHa
www.brewhahatea.co.uk

Lahloo Tea
www.lahlootea.co.uk

Mad Hatter Tea
www.madhattertea.co.uk

Steenbergs Organics
www.steenbergs.co.uk

Tea Adventures
www.tea-adventure.com

Tea Experience
www.teaexperience.co.uk

Tea Horse
www.teahorse.co.uk

The Tea Palace
www.teapalace.co.uk

The Rare Tea Company
www.rareteacompany.com

Trumpers Tea
www.trumperstea.co.uk

Waterloo Tea
www.waterlootea.com

Organic Teas, Teapots and Cups
www.teasme.co.uk

All You Need to Bake the Perfect Afternoon Tea

www.lakeland.co.uk

Afternoon Tea Reservations

The Ritz
+44 (0)20 7300 2345

The Merrion, Dublin
+353 1 603 0600

Bettys *- Reservations can be made for either the Harrogate or York Tearooms*

Harrogate: +44 (0)1423 814070

York: +44 (0)1904 659142

The Balmoral, Edinburgh
+44 131 556 2414

Find a Tea Room Near You
www.tearoomsdirectory.co.uk

For More Information on Tea in Britain

The Tea Council
www.tea.co.uk

Tea Masterclasses
www.janepettigrew.com/ masterclass

Photo Credits

Page 7, 21 Tregothnan Tea, Cornwall

Page 16, 17 The Ritz, London

Page 17 Fortnum and Mason, London

Page 23, 24, 32 Bettys and Taylors of Harrogate

Page 24 Howick Hall and Gardens, Northumberland

Page 25 Ringtons Tea

Page 28 The Merrion Hotel, Dublin

Page 41 Rudding Park, Harrogate

Page 45 Green's Restaurant, Whitby

Pages 9,12,13,

4,29,33,57 istock

Cover and all other images by Ron Blenkinsop